Introduction

This book is meant for use as a short reference guide for research design. It is double-spaced for you to make notes on the book itself. Many students need help with this part of the dissertation process as they think about their topic and formulate a research question. This is more like a short research design handbook to refer to early in the dissertation development process. It helps you get started and will be helpful throughout your dissertation writing process.

Table of Contents

<u>Chapter 1: First Steps for getting started on a Dissertation</u>

You have finally finished coursework in your master's or doctoral program. Now it is time to start a significant research project supporting a dissertation or a thesis, and you have no idea where to start. This guide will help you think through the most common methods used in research to help you think through the process and choose the best fit for your academic study. We will use the dissertation process for this book, although it can be used for a shorter thesis in a master's program.

Starting a dissertation can be overwhelming, but here are some steps you can take to get started:

- Choose a topic: Start by identifying a topic that interests you, and you feel passionate about. Next, consider topics relevant to your field of study that you have some prior knowledge of.

- Conduct a literature review: A literature review can help you identify gaps in the existing research that your dissertation can address. Read widely and critically to identify your area of interest's key themes, debates, and controversies.

- Develop a research question: Based on your literature review, develop a research question that is clear, concise, and manageable. Your research question should be focused enough to be answered within the scope of your dissertation.

- Determine your research methodology: Choose one appropriate for your research question and align it with your objectives. Qualitative, quantitative, or mixed methods are some options you can consider.

- Develop a research plan: Develop a research plan that outlines the steps you need to take to collect and analyze your data. This plan should include details about your research design, data collection methods, sampling strategy, data analysis techniques, and ethical considerations.

Conducting a dissertation is a process, and it may take time to refine your research question, collect your data, and analyze your findings.

The first step is to determine your research topic and read, read, read! You need to do much reading on your topic before settling on a research question. Follow these steps for a clear and focused research question:

- Start with a broad area of interest: Begin by identifying a vast area that aligns with your field of study and your interests. For example, if you are studying psychology, you may be interested in the relationship between mental health and social media use.

- Conduct a literature review: Conduct a comprehensive literature review to identify the key themes, debates, and controversies in your area of interest. This will help you to refine your research question and identify gaps in the existing research that your dissertation can address.

- Refine your area of interest: Based on your literature review, refine your area of interest and identify a specific research problem or question you want to investigate. Your research question should be clear, concise, manageable, and reflect your interests and expertise.

- Consider the feasibility of your research question: Consider the feasibility of your research question in terms of your available resources, the time frame for your dissertation, and ethical considerations. Ensure that your research question is realistic and achievable within the scope of your dissertation.

Quantitative research is used in all fields to study many phenomena, including social, behavioral, educational, medical, and business-related issues. In this chapter, we review the types and offer examples of each.

Descriptive quantitative research

Descriptive quantitative research is a methodology used to describe or summarize characteristics or phenomena of interest. It involves collecting and analyzing numerical data through surveys, questionnaires, and statistical analysis.

This type of research aims to portray a phenomenon or group accurately and objectively. It does not seek to establish causality or relationships between variables but rather to describe the characteristics of a population or a particular phenomenon.

Examples include surveys that gather data on demographic characteristics such as age, gender, income, and education level, or studies that describe the prevalence and incidence of a particular disease or health condition in a population. This research may also involve statistical methods to summarize and analyze the data collected. These methods may include measures of central tendency such as mean, median, and mode or variability such as standard deviation and range.

A descriptive quantitative research study uses numerical data to describe or summarize a particular phenomenon or group. This type of research aims to provide an accurate and objective portrayal of a population or a specific phenomenon without attempting to establish causality or relationships between variables.

An example of a descriptive quantitative research study could be a survey to gather information about public opinions and attitudes toward a particular social issue. For instance, a researcher may conduct a study to understand public perceptions of climate change. The researcher would design a survey questionnaire to gather data on public opinions about climate change. For example, the questionnaire might include questions about knowledge, attitudes, and willingness to act in support of climate change. The survey would be distributed to a sample of the population of interest, such as adults in a particular country or region. The data collected would be analyzed using statistical methods to identify patterns, trends, and relationships between variables.

The survey results would provide a descriptive summary of public opinions and attitudes toward climate change. For example, the study might reveal that a significant proportion of the population believes climate change is a severe problem and that there is widespread support for government action to address the issue. The study's findings could be used to inform policy decisions related to climate change and to develop targeted communication and education strategies to increase public awareness and engagement around the issue.

A descriptive quantitative research study collects and analyzes numerical data to describe or summarize a particular phenomenon or group. In the example of a survey on public attitudes towards climate change, the goal is to provide a descriptive summary of public opinions and attitudes towards climate change, which can be used to inform policy decisions and communication strategies.

Correlational quantitative research

A correlational quantitative research study is a research methodology used to examine the relationship between two or more variables. This type of research aims to determine whether there is a statistical relationship between variables and, if so, the strength and direction of that relationship. This method involves collecting numerical data, typically through surveys, experiments, or other quantitative methods. Then, the data is analyzed using statistical techniques to determine the degree of association between the variables of interest. Correlational research does not establish causality but identifies the degree to which two or more variables are related. It is important to note that a correlation does not necessarily imply causation, as other factors may influence the relationship between the variables.

An example of a correlational quantitative research study could be investigating the relationship between exercise and mental health. The researcher might collect data on the number of hours of exercise per week and measures of mental health, such as anxiety and depression scores, for a sample of participants.

The data collected would be analyzed using statistical techniques such as correlation coefficients, revealing the degree of association between the two variables. For example, the study's results might show a significant correlation between exercise and mental health, indicating that people who exercise more tend to have better mental health outcomes. The method is used to examine the relationship between two or more variables. It involves collecting and analyzing numerical data to identify the degree of association between variables of interest. However, it is important to remember that a correlation does not necessarily imply causation.

An example of a correlational research study could be investigating the relationship between smoking and lung cancer. The researcher might collect data on smoking behavior and the incidence of lung cancer for a sample of participants. Then, the data collected would be analyzed using statistical techniques such as correlation coefficients, revealing the degree of association between the two variables. For example, the study's results might show a significant positive correlation between smoking and lung cancer, indicating that people who smoke more tend to have higher lung cancer rates. Another example of a correlational research study could be investigating the relationship between academic achievement and parental involvement. For example, the researcher might collect data on parental involvement in a child's education, such as attending parent-teacher conferences and helping with homework, as well as the child's academic achievement, such as grades and standardized test scores. Then, the data collected could be analyzed using statistical techniques to determine the degree of association between parental involvement and academic achievement. For example, the study's results might show a significant positive correlation between parental involvement and academic achievement, indicating that children whose parents are more involved in their education tend to have higher academic achievement.

In both examples, the correlational research study aims to examine the relationship between two variables, and the study results can provide valuable information about the strength and direction of that relationship. However, it is important to note that correlation does not necessarily imply causation, as other factors may influence the relationship between the variables.

A systematic review

A systematic review is a research study that identifies, appraises, and synthesizes all available evidence on a specific research question or topic. It involves a rigorous and systematic approach to searching, selecting, and analyzing existing studies to provide a comprehensive and unbiased summary of the research findings.

Systematic reviews typically involve the following steps:

- Defining the research question or topic

- Developing a comprehensive search strategy to identify relevant studies

- Screening and selecting studies based on predetermined inclusion and exclusion criteria

- Assessing the quality of the included studies using established criteria

- Extracting data from the included studies

- Synthesizing the findings of the included studies, often using statistical methods or meta-analysis

- Drawing conclusions and making recommendations based on the evidence gathered.

- Systematic reviews are often used in healthcare, medicine, and other fields where evidence-based decision-making is essential. They provide a high level of evidence and are considered one of the most reliable sources of information for making informed decisions about interventions, policies, or practices.

It is important to note that this method can be quantitative or qualitative, depending on the data being analyzed.

Quasi-experimental research

Quasi-experimental research is a methodology used to study cause-and-effect relationships between variables. In quasi-experimental research, the investigator does not have complete control over the experimental conditions, as would be true in a proper experimental design. Instead, the study is conducted naturally, often with pre-existing groups or conditions. This method manipulates an independent variable to observe its effect on a dependent variable. However, unlike in true experimental designs, the groups are not randomly assigned to conditions, making it difficult to establish causality with certainty. Quasi-experimental research designs often use statistical techniques to control for potential confounding variables and increase the study's internal validity.

An example of quasi-experimental research could be a study examining the effectiveness of a new teaching strategy on student performance in a specific subject. For example, the researcher might identify two groups of students from different schools, one given the new teaching strategy and the other not. The researcher then measures the student's performance in both groups on a specific exam. However, since the groups were not randomly assigned, pre-existing differences between the two groups may have affected the results. To address this issue, the researcher might use statistical techniques to control for potential confounding variables, such as previous academic performance or socio-economic status.

In summary, quasi-experimental research is a research methodology used to study cause-and-effect relationships between variables in a natural setting. Unlike true experimental designs, quasi-experimental designs do not randomly assign participants to conditions, making it difficult to establish causality with certainty. Quasi-experimental research designs often use statistical techniques to control for potential confounding variables to increase the study's internal validity.

Another example of a quasi-experimental research study could be a study examining the effect of a new drug on blood pressure levels in patients with hypertension. In this case, the researcher could identify two groups of patients, one receiving the new drug and the other receiving the standard treatment for hypertension. However, since the groups were not randomly assigned, pre-existing differences between the two groups may have also affected the results in this case.

To address this issue, the researcher might use statistical techniques to control for potential confounding variables, such as age, sex, and baseline blood pressure levels. For example, the researcher could match the participants in the two groups based on these variables or use statistical analysis methods like regression or analysis of covariance (ANCOVA) to account for these differences. The researcher would then measure the blood pressure levels of the participants in both groups at regular intervals and compare the results. If the results show that the new drug significantly affects blood pressure levels, this could suggest that it may be an effective treatment for hypertension.

Experimental Research

Experimental research is a research methodology used to study cause-and-effect relationships between variables in a controlled setting. In experimental research, the researcher manipulates an independent variable and observes its effect on a dependent variable while controlling for potential confounding variables. In an experimental study, participants are randomly assigned to different groups or conditions, each receiving a different level or version of the independent variable. The researcher then measures the effect of the independent variable on the dependent variable.

Experimental research designs are the gold standard because they allow researchers to establish causality between variables. By controlling for potential confounding variables and manipulating the independent variable, the researcher can more confidently conclude that the independent variable caused the observed changes in the dependent variable.

An example of an experimental research study could be a study examining the effect of a new medication on pain management. The researcher might randomly assign participants to two groups, one receiving the latest medicines and the other receiving a placebo. The researcher would then measure the participants' pain levels regularly and compare the results between the two groups. If the results show that the new medication significantly affects pain levels, this could suggest that it may be an effective treatment for pain management.

Chapter 3: Which quantitative method should I use for my research?

Choosing the best quantitative research method for your study depends on several factors, including the research question, the data you want to collect, the resources available, and the level of precision you need. Here are some steps you can follow in choosing the best quantitative research method for your study:

Start by clearly defining your research question. This will help you determine the type of data you need to collect and the research method that is most appropriate for answering your question.

Next, consider the kind of data you need to collect. Do you need numerical data or categorical data? This is quantitative data. Do you need data on attitudes, behaviors, or opinions? This would be considered qualitative. Understanding this will help you determine the appropriate method for collecting your data. You should proceed with quantitative methods if you choose numerical or categorical data.

Consider the resources available, including time, budget, and personnel. Some research methods require more resources, so choosing a feasible method is crucial, given your resources.

Review the literature to see what other researchers have done with similar research questions. This can give you an idea of the methods used successfully. Next, select the appropriate research design that suits your research question. The research design will determine the research method to use. Next, consider the level of precision you need in your data. If you need a high level of precision, you may need to use a more complex research method. Finally, it is always wise to seek advice from experts in your field or consult with a research methodologist to guide you on the best research method.

Overall, the best quantitative research method for your study will depend on the specific details of your research question, data, resources, and precision level. Therefore, it is crucial to take the time to carefully evaluate your options before making a final decision.

<u>**Chapter 4: Types of qualitative research methods and their application**</u>

Qualitative research explores and attempts to understand phenomena of a social nature. In this chapter, we will review the types and offer examples.

Thematic analysis

Thematic analysis is a flexible method that can be applied to a wide range of research questions and qualitative data types. It involves a systematic and rigorous approach to analyzing qualitative data to identify patterns, themes, and meanings, which can help researchers gain a deeper understanding of the phenomena under investigation. For example, it is often used in social sciences, such as psychology, sociology, and anthropology, to analyze interview transcripts, focus group discussions, or other forms of qualitative data.

An example of thematic analysis could be analyzing the experiences of individuals who have undergone weight loss surgery. Researchers conducting the thematic analysis might interview a sample of individuals who have undergone weight loss surgery and ask them about their experiences before, during, and after the surgery. After conducting the interviews, the researchers would transcribe and analyze the data using thematic analysis. They might generate initial codes that capture the key ideas and concepts in the data, such as the physical and emotional challenges of the surgery, the impact on social relationships, and the role of support networks. The researchers would then group the initial codes into broader themes based on similarities or differences. For example, they might group codes related to physical challenges into a theme called "Managing Physical Changes" and codes about emotional challenges into a theme called "Coping with Emotional Changes."

After refining the themes, the researchers would define and name each theme, write a report presenting the themes, and provide examples from the data to support each theme. For example, the report might reveal everyday experiences among individuals who have undergone weight loss surgery, such as the challenges of adjusting to physical changes and the importance of social support networks. These findings could inform the development of interventions to support individuals undergoing weight loss surgery.

Content analysis

This type of research is used to analyze text, images, or other forms of media. It involves coding and categorizing the content to identify themes, patterns, and trends. It can be used to identify themes, patterns, and trends. It involves a systematic approach to examining the content of a particular medium, such as books, newspapers, social media posts, or advertisements, and analyzing the patterns and themes that emerge.

Content analysis can be used to study a wide range of research questions, including the representation of certain groups in the media, the portrayal of specific topics, or the prevalence of certain attitudes or behaviors. Researchers use content analysis to examine the content of the media and draw inferences about the underlying social, cultural, or political messages being conveyed.

There are two main approaches to content analysis: manifest content analysis and latent content analysis. Manifest content analysis involves identifying the visible, surface-level characteristics of the media, such as the frequency of certain words or images. Latent content analysis, on the other hand, involves identifying the underlying meanings, assumptions, or values that are being conveyed through the media.

An example of content analysis could be analyzing the representation of women in advertising. This could involve collecting a sample of print or online advertisements and examining how women are depicted in the images and messages conveyed in the ads. For example, the content analysis might involve coding the advertisements based on the following variables: the number of female and male characters, the portrayal of female characters as passive or active, the types of products advertised to women, and the use of stereotypical gender roles or sexualized images. The researcher could then analyze the data to identify patterns and trends in the representation of women in advertising.

For example, the analysis might reveal that women are more likely to be depicted in passive roles or as sexual objects in certain advertisements, such as those for beauty products or fashion. These findings could inform our understanding of how advertising perpetuates gender stereotypes and contribute to efforts to promote more gender-equitable representations in media.

Overall, content analysis is a valuable research method for analyzing large volumes of media to identify patterns and themes that can inform our understanding of social, cultural, or political issues.

Phenomenological qualitative research

Phenomenological qualitative research is an approach to qualitative research that focuses on the lived experiences of individuals or groups. It involves profoundly exploring the subjective experiences and meanings of the phenomenon being studied, as described by the participants. Phenomenological research aims to understand the essence of a phenomenon or how the participants experience it. This is achieved through in-depth interviews or other qualitative data collection methods. The researcher encourages participants to describe their experiences in as much detail as possible and to reflect on the meaning of those experiences.

Phenomenological research is typically used in social sciences, psychology, nursing, and other fields where subjective experiences and meaning-making are essential areas of study. In addition, it is often used to explore health, illness, emotions, spirituality, and human relationships.

An example of phenomenological qualitative research could be a study investigating the experience of living with chronic pain. The researcher might conduct in-depth interviews with individuals living with chronic pain for an extended period, asking them to describe their experiences in detail. The interviews might explore the participants' experiences of pain, including the physical sensations, the emotional impact, and the effect on their daily lives. The researcher would encourage participants to reflect on their experiences' meaning and describe their subjective perceptions and interpretations of their pain. The data collected from the interviews would then be analyzed using a phenomenological approach, which involves identifying the common themes and essential structures of the participants' experiences.

The study's findings could provide a deep understanding of the essence of living with chronic pain, including the unique and subjective ways individuals experience and interpret their pain. This information could inform healthcare practices and policies to support better individuals living with

chronic pain, including developing new treatment approaches and

interventions tailored to everyone's unique experiences.

Descriptive qualitative research

Descriptive qualitative research is a research method that focuses on

describing and interpreting the phenomenon being studied rather than

explaining it. This type of qualitative research seeks to provide an in-depth

understanding of the topic under investigation by exploring the participants'

experiences, beliefs, and perspectives.

In descriptive qualitative research, the researcher collects data through

various methods such as interviews, observation, focus groups, and document

analysis. Then, the data collected is analyzed using content, thematic, and

narrative analysis.

The main goal of descriptive qualitative research is to provide a rich

and detailed description of the phenomenon being studied, including its

context, the participants' experiences, and the meanings they attach to it. It is

often used in social sciences, education, health, and psychology, where a

detailed understanding of human experiences and behaviors is important. This

method can be used as a stand-alone research method or as part of a larger mixed-methods research design, providing a more comprehensive and nuanced understanding of the phenomenon being studied.

An example of descriptive qualitative research could be a study investigating the experiences of individuals recently diagnosed with a chronic illness such as diabetes. The researcher might conduct in-depth interviews with participants, asking them open-ended questions about their experiences receiving the diagnosis, their emotions and reactions, their perceptions of the impact on their life, and their coping strategies. The data collected from the interviews would then be analyzed using qualitative data analysis techniques such as content analysis or thematic analysis to identify common themes and patterns in the participants' experiences.

The study's findings could then provide a detailed understanding of the subjective experiences of individuals living with diabetes, including their emotional responses, challenges, and strategies to manage their illness. This information could better inform healthcare practices and policies to support individuals with chronic diseases.

Narrative qualitative research

Narrative qualitative research is a research method that involves collecting and analyzing stories or narratives from individuals about their personal experiences. This approach focuses on understanding individuals'

meanings and interpretations of their experiences rather than identifying

specific themes or patterns. This method typically involves collecting data

through interviews or other oral or written storytelling forms, such as diaries

or letters. Then, the data is analyzed using qualitative data analysis techniques

such as narrative analysis, which involves identifying the narrative structure,

content, and themes.

Narrative qualitative research aims to gain a rich and detailed

understanding of how individuals experience and make sense of their lives and

the world around them. This method is often used in psychology, sociology,

and anthropology to study identity, culture, and social change.

An example of narrative qualitative research could be a study

investigating the experiences of refugees who have resettled in a new country.

The researcher might interview refugees, asking them to tell their stories of

leaving their home country, their journey to the new country, and their

experiences of resettling and adapting to a new culture. Then, the collected

narratives would be analyzed using narrative analysis to identify common

themes and patterns in the refugees' experiences and to understand their

perspectives on displacement, resettlement, and belonging.

Case study qualitative research

Case study qualitative research is a research method that focuses on in-depth investigation and analysis of a single individual, group, or event. The case study approach aims to provide a detailed and comprehensive understanding of the case being studied by exploring the context, history, and unique characteristics. This method involves collecting data from multiple sources, such as interviews, observations, and documents, to build a rich and detailed picture of the studied case. The data is then analyzed using qualitative techniques such as content or thematic analysis.

Case studies are often used in fields such as psychology, sociology, and education, where a detailed understanding of individual experiences and behaviors is essential. In addition, case study research is beneficial when the case being studied is rare, complex, or difficult to replicate or when the focus is on understanding the unique features of a particular case.

An example of case study qualitative research could be a study investigating a student's experiences with a learning disability in a particular school. The researcher might interview the student, their teachers, and their parents, observe the student in the classroom and review their academic records. The data collected would be analyzed to identify the unique features of the student's experience, their challenges, and the strategies that have successfully supported their learning. The study findings could then inform policies and practices for supporting students with learning disabilities in similar contexts.

Grounded Theory

Grounded theory is a research methodology developed by sociologists Barney Glaser and Anselm Strauss in the 1960s. The main idea behind grounded theory is to develop a theory or explanation of a phenomenon by systematically collecting and analyzing data.

Unlike traditional research methods, grounded theory is not based on a pre-existing theory or hypothesis. Instead, the theory emerges from the data collected during the research process. This means that researchers approach the data with an open mind and are willing to revise or refine their theory based on what they learn from the data.

The process of grounded theory research typically involves several stages, including data collection, coding, categorization, and theoretical sampling. First, researchers may use various data collection methods, such as interviews, observations, and surveys, to collect data on the phenomenon they are studying. They then analyze the data by coding it or breaking it down into smaller parts and categorizing it based on similarities and differences.

As the research progresses, the researchers may refine their categories and conduct additional interviews or observations to gather more data on specific aspects of the phenomenon. Through this process of theoretical sampling and refinement, a theory that explains the phenomenon being studied begins to emerge.

Grounded theory research is often used in social sciences, such as sociology, psychology, and anthropology, but it can be applied to any field that involves understanding complex phenomena.

Action qualitative research

Action qualitative research is a specific approach to qualitative research characterized by its focus on social action and social change. This approach is often used in social justice research, community-based research, and participatory research, where the goal is not only to understand a particular social issue but also to take action to address it.

Action qualitative research involves engaging with participants and stakeholders to identify the most pressing social issues and then working collaboratively to develop strategies and interventions that address these issues. The research process is iterative, and findings are often used to inform ongoing action and change.

Action qualitative research is a research approach that seeks to create meaningful change by involving participants in the research process and using findings to inform action and social change.

An example of qualitative action research would be a study conducted in a low-income community to identify and address issues related to food insecurity. The research team might work collaboratively with community members, including residents, community organizations, and businesses, to determine the area's root causes of food insecurity. The research team might use qualitative methods such as interviews, focus groups, and observations to gather data on the experiences and perspectives of community members related to food insecurity. They might also conduct a thorough review of existing research on the topic.

Using this data, the research team would work collaboratively with the community to develop strategies and interventions to address food insecurity. For example, they might work with local businesses to increase the availability of healthy and affordable food options or with community organizations to provide education and resources to help individuals and families access nutritious food.

Throughout the research process, the community would be actively involved in shaping the research questions, interpreting the findings, and developing strategies for action. The research would not only seek to understand the problem of food insecurity but also to create meaningful and practical solutions for the community.

Ethnographic qualitative research

Ethnographic qualitative research is a methodology involving systematically studying people and cultures in their natural settings. This approach is commonly used in the social sciences, particularly anthropology, sociology, and education.

Ethnographic research involves observing and interacting with individuals and groups in their natural environments over a prolonged period. The researcher immerses themselves in the culture being studied and seeks to understand the beliefs, values, practices, and behaviors of the people within that culture.

Data collection methods in ethnographic research may include participant observation, in-depth interviews, focus groups, and analysis of cultural artifacts such as photographs, documents, and videos. In addition, ethnographic research often involves building close relationships with the people being studied, which can lead to rich, in-depth insights into their experiences and perspectives.

Ethnographic qualitative research can be used to investigate a wide range of social phenomena, such as cultural practices, social norms, and social institutions. It is often used to explore the experiences of marginalized groups, such as immigrant communities or people living in poverty, and to investigate social issues such as inequality, power dynamics, and social change.

In summary, qualitative ethnographic research is a research approach that involves the systematic study of people and cultures in their natural settings, using methods such as participant observation and in-depth interviews to gain rich insights into the beliefs, values, practices, and behaviors of the people being studied.

An example of ethnographic research could be a study conducted to understand a specific community's social and cultural practices. For instance, a researcher may conduct an ethnographic study of a rural community to understand the beliefs, values, and practices surrounding health and healing. The researcher would immerse themselves in the community, observing and participating in the daily life of the community members. They would conduct in-depth interviews with community members, such as healers, local doctors, and patients, to understand their experiences and perspectives on health and healing. The researcher may also observe traditional healing practices and rituals, such as herbal remedies, spiritual practices, or traditional ceremonies. In addition, they may analyze cultural artifacts such as traditional medicines and medical texts to understand the history and evolution of the community's health practices.

The data collected through the ethnographic research would be analyzed to identify patterns, themes, and insights that emerge from the experiences and perspectives of the community members. The researcher would then use these insights to deeply understand the community's health practices and make recommendations for improving health outcomes.

An ethnographic research study involves immersing oneself in a specific community or culture to understand the people's beliefs, values, and practices. This type of research is used to gain rich insights into a particular group's social and cultural traditions and can be applied to a wide range of research topics.

You decided the best research design would be qualitative based on the data you require to answer your research question. Now what?

- Choosing the correct qualitative research method depends on the research question, the nature of the phenomenon being studied, and the research objectives. Here are some steps to consider when choosing a qualitative research method:

- Begin by clarifying the research question you want to answer. This will help you determine the type of data you need to collect and the research method most suitable.

- Consider the characteristics of the phenomenon you are studying, including its complexity, uniqueness, and depth. For example, some research methods may be more appropriate for studying complex or dynamic phenomena, while others may be better suited for studying more straightforward phenomena.

- Different qualitative research methods have strengths and weaknesses. For example, ethnographic research is well-suited for studying cultural practices, while grounded theory helps develop theories grounded in empirical data.

- Consider practical topics such as time, resources, and participant access. For example, some research methods may require more time and resources than others, and some may require access to specific populations or settings.
- Ensure that the research method you choose is ethical and protects the rights and well-being of the participants.
- Consult with experts in qualitative research to get their perspectives and advice on the most appropriate research method for your research question.

Choosing the best research design can be difficult at first, but once you have identified a topic and formulated a research question, you must consider the type of data that will best answer the research question(s). This is the most crucial step in the entire process because the study will only be valid if the data you collect adequately addresses the research question.

For example, if you want to examine the experiences of new mothers during the COVID-19 pandemic, you would not be able to find answers that address that with numerical data. Therefore, be exhaustive in your review of research methods and make sure that the research design and methods are the best fit for your study, and you will be able to provide a solid structure for your research study!